surviving & thriving *with* ASPERGER'S

Stories & Tools To Help You Relax, Communicate, and Navigate The World

By Asperger Experts

Copyright © 2020 Asperger Experts LLC.

All rights reserved. No part of this publication may be reproduced, distributed, or transmitted in any form or by any means, including photocopying, recording, or other electronic or mechanical methods, without the prior written permission of the publisher, except in the case of brief quotations embodied in critical reviews and certain other noncommercial uses permitted by copyright law. For permission requests, please email us at help@aspergerexperts.com

> Asperger Experts LLC
> help@aspergerexperts.com
> www.AspergerExperts.com

Special discounts are available on quantity purchases by corporations, associations, and others. For details, contact us at help@aspergerexperts.com

Surviving and Thriving with Asperger's: Stories and Tools to Help You Relax, Communicate, and Navigate the World/Asperger Experts. —1st ed.

ISBN 978-1-945611-04-9

TABLE OF CONTENTS

Part 1: Self
Introduction 7
Definition of Asperger's 11
My Story 19
Picky Eating 27
Hygiene 33

Part 2: Emotional Capacity
Defense Mode 37
Stress and Self-Care 45

Part 3: The Outside World
Stories, Perspectives and Getting Help 61
Moving Your Life Forward 69

Conclusion 73

PART 1:
Self

Introduction

TIME TO BE REAL WITH YOU. Sometimes, life with Asperger's can suck. A lot.

Whether you are raising someone on the spectrum, are on the spectrum yourself, or both, there are times when you're going to be disappointed. There are times when you're going to be extremely frustrated. There are times when you don't know how on earth you are going to continue, because it feels like your entire world is falling apart before your very eyes.

There are times where you are so anxious that you feel like you're going to die.

I've had all of those moments and then some. My name is Danny Raede, and I was diagnosed with Asperger's when I was twelve. Since 2012, I've been running Asperger Experts full time. It's a company that is equally based in the personal experience of having Asperger's, the latest science and cutting edge research, and the experience of working professionally with, at the time of writing this, over five hundred thousand people.

So yes, this is hard sometimes, and the problem is compounded because the world is not set up for people with Asperger's. It's hard enough for neurotypical people to live in the world, and it is just that much harder for people with Asperger's to go about living in a way that works well for them and gives them joy and fulfillment.

But it doesn't have to be that way forever. In fact, once you understand some basic ideas, gain some necessary tools, and implement some effective strategies, life can be as enjoyable as you want it to be, Asperger's or not.

What you hold in your hands is both a story of how I managed to build an enjoyable life, despite having Asperger's and ADD, and a toolkit that gives you extremely simple and actionable information, tools, and resources so that you, too, can live a fulfilling life.

As I was growing up, most of the time I was really shut down. I was in Defense Mode constantly, and I didn't have many friends. So I spent my time playing video games, browsing the internet, and waiting. I did a lot of waiting. Waiting until I could play more video games, waiting until the weekend. Waiting until I felt less lonely.

I'll tell my story in-depth later in this book, but if you fast-forward about a decade, I co-created Asperger Experts because I found the amount of helpful information targeted toward people with Asperger's to be extremely limited. So I decided to do the work to find, create, research, and document that information instead of continuing to wait.

Throughout the years that we've been running AE, we've noticed a pattern in all of the interactions we've had. People come up to us and say, "I'm confused, and I'm frustrated. Help."

That is usually followed by a story of an injustice they've experienced in their life. We've heard horror stories about teachers locking kids in broom closets because they misbehave, or bullies badly abusing kids on the spectrum. We've seen what happens when people on the spectrum become lonely and depressed.

The point is, you aren't alone on this journey. Here at AE, sadly, we know the horrors that you have experienced. We know that the world mistreats you often and dismisses you.

PART ONE: SELF

Here at AE, we live with Asperger's every single day. We don't get to go home at the end of the day and turn off work. This is life. This is what we do.

We are here for you. And we're going to do our darn best to listen to you, to hear you, to really understand your struggles, to validate your pain, and to give you a voice to spread the message to other people. That is what we're here for.

Our number one job is to make sure that you get our best, to make sure that you actually feel heard, to make sure that you get the answers to the help that you are seeking, and to make sure that you don't always need to feel that gnawing, anxious, "Oh my God, oh God, oh, what am I going to do?" feeling.

Above all else, we're here to help you actually get some real answers from real people that know what they're talking about because they have been through it. People that can put their arm around your shoulder and say, "Hey, I've been here, too. It's OK. Let me show you where to go from here."

Our job here is to be in the trenches with you, because we are. We get it. It sucks sometimes. But you know what? You aren't a bad person. None of this is your fault. It is unfortunately common to hear stories of other people saying to people on the spectrum, "You are just being willfully defiant and not trying hard enough!"

Now of course, that is complete BS, and none of that is true. They forget the fact that if you're living in a system that traumatizes you, where people yell at you and the school system dismisses you, then the normal response to that would be to shut down because that is scary. That's just traumatizing. That causes fear.

So that's not how we roll around here. We see you for you. And I want to make that really, really clear, so you can expect our best here at AE. You can expect that guidance. You can expect that help. You can expect somebody to listen because we've all been through the stuff together.

If you'd like to share your story and participate in our community, we invite you to create a free account at www.AspergerExperts.com. With that being said, lets get started.

How to Use This Book

People with Asperger's (like myself) often have a component of ADD that comes along with the diagnosis. It is hard for us to focus for long periods of time, especially on things that are heavy and talk about life (like this book). So I've decided to embrace that trait.

This isn't a "read front to back" kind of book. I encourage you to be ADD and skip around! Find the sections that interest you and read those. Ignore the rest if you want to. Come back often because you'll find that your perspective changes, and what was once boring and irrelevant becomes interesting over time, and vice-versa.

Definition of Asperger's

What Is Asperger's Anyway?

Asperger's is a neurological condition that causes a person to become overwhelmed by their sensations, be unable to connect socially with their peers, and start to withdraw into a world of their own creation. Now if you ask a doctor, the term Asperger's has actually been phased out and it's now been replaced with Autism Spectrum Disorder. At least according to the "Diagnostic And Statistical Manual of Mental Disorders (DSM-5)" (Isn't that a friendly and pleasant name!)

But it essentially means the same thing. It's just a different label. We continue to use the word Asperger's because it still holds a lot of meaning for people. They still identify with it, and they still know what it stands for .

To us, the difference between someone with Asperger's and a neurotypical (someone who has a "typical" or average nervous system) is like the difference between a Mac and a PC. They're both computers. They can both access Google. There are slight differences in hardware and software between the two, but they both accomplish most of the same functions.

The icons may be slightly moved, things may work a little differently, and there may be distinct workflow steps to get to the same function, but it's all still there and it all still works. Each type is just for different kinds of people.

Many individuals ask for specific advice when it comes to those with Asperger's, such as "What school is best for someone with Asperger's?" But that's like asking the question "What type of school is good for someone with blond hair?"

That's not a question you would ask, because people with blond hair are people, people with Asperger's are people. We just have a different way of looking at the world.

Let's go deeper and break down that definition of Asperger's that I gave you at the beginning. We'll start with a "neurological difference." The key word here is "difference." It is not a disease. There is nothing contagious about it. It is not something that's wrong. It is literally just a different way of thinking and being in the world.

Technically, Asperger's is a "syndrome," which just means "a group of symptoms." A symptom is just another way of saying there's a set of behaviors, actions, or effects that we are going to group together. So in reality, Asperger's isn't anything more than a different way of existing in the world.

The second part of our definition sentence is "overwhelmed by sensation." That means we are constantly shut down because there is way too much input coming in. Sights, sounds, smells, touch, taste, and the internal felt sense of our various bodily systems all work together to inform our understanding of the world, but people with Asperger's can't handle and process all of that information adequately.

Overwhelmed by sensation also means that we are in Defense Mode a lot. Defense Mode is a state where we are disconnected and extremely overwhelmed and literally terrified of everything. In scientific terms, that means we have low vagal tone and faulty neuroception.

PART ONE: SELF

We'll talk in much more depth about Defense Mode in the "Defense Mode" section of this book.

The next part of our sentence is "be unable to connect socially." People with Asperger's are usually unable to connect socially in a meaningful way. And since a large part of being able to emotionally regulate and be a successful contributor to society depends on your ability to form and keep meaningful relationships in your life, those on the autism spectrum tend to greatly struggle with this area.

The last part of the sentence is "withdraw into a world of their own creation." What that means is that, due to Defense Mode, low vagal tone, and faulty neuroception like we discussed briefly, the actual world sometimes seems too threatening and too scary, so we tend to withdraw into our own world and become over focused on and overspecialized in one thing.

As a result of this, we become really, really good at our expert topic, but largely unable to function to varying degrees outside of our specialty.

As I said earlier, at the end of the day Asperger's is just a label. It's a word used to describe a whole bunch of symptoms like anxiety, depression, lack of social skills, and obsession. That's it. That's all there is. It's just a label. It's like saying, "I'm standing in a collection of brick and glass and steel and stone," rather than in a building.

It's not a defect. There is no moral failing. It's just a different way of seeing and participating in the world. Nothing is "wrong" here.

And when you understand that, nothing changes. . . . And everything changes. You stop seeing yourself as something that is broken that needs to be fixed, and you start seeing yourself as a whole, valid human who just needs to find their place in the world.

Sensory Funnel

This is The Sensory Funnel, and it describes how Asperger's works.

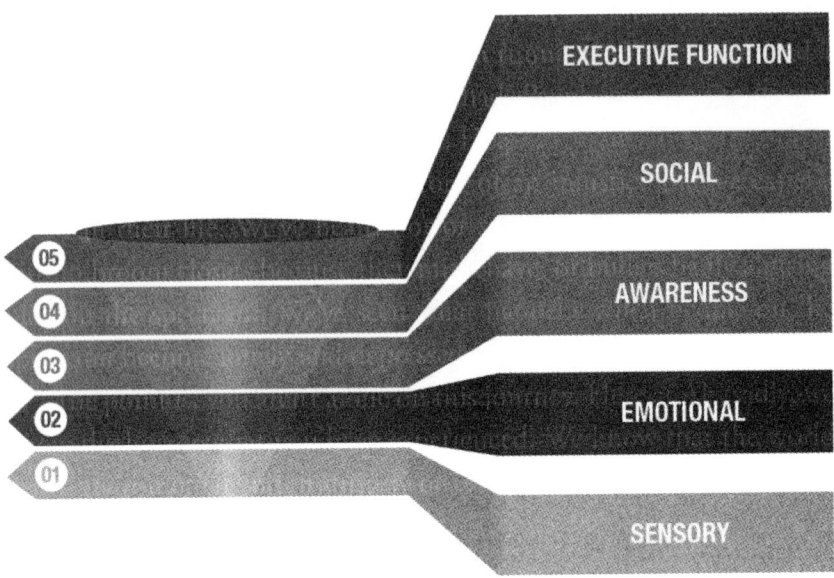

The biggest problem we see is that most of the parents, teachers, therapists, and people on the spectrum tend to focus on the top part of the funnel, the executive function and the social skills issues, while completely ignoring the rest.

Here's the thing: The rest of the funnel—the sensory issues, the emotional component, and the awareness piece . . . those are the most important part. That's what really matters. If you work on the bottom three pieces, I've found that the social skills and executive functioning pieces either resolve themselves or become extremely easy to resolve.

PART ONE: SELF

So let's break down The Sensory Funnel starting with the bottom. When I say "sensory," I mean the five senses, like sight and smell, but also the internal visceral sensations such as your heart beating and your gut gurgling

I also mean the sensory component to emotional states, for example, if you have anxiety and you can physically feel your throat closing and your chest tightening. Or when you feel gratitude and there's a warm sensation going through your body.

The problem is that all of these sensory inputs really overwhelm a lot of people with Asperger's, shut them down, and put them into Defense Mode.

And then we get the emotional issues layered on top of the sensory issues, which further compound things. Now not only do you have overwhelm from a sensation, you also have anxiety about a sensation happening again.

Then it gets further compounded by depression: you have anger, shame, and associated emotional issues.

Because of all of these overwhelming issues, you're in Defense Mode so deep that you constantly feel like you're being attacked from everywhere. Then your awareness shuts down, and you hide and wait.

This may not be your exact experience as someone on the spectrum, but from the thousands of people with Asperger's I've personally talked to, I bet it's darn close!

Anyway, then comes the awareness piece. In short: the more Defense Mode you have, the less you are aware of yourself, where you are in space (think coordination), and your impact on others.

Now, finally, we get to the social skills piece. "Asperger's is a social-skills deficit," they say. "Let's teach them social skills," they exclaim.

Think for a moment about how you learned the social skills you do have. For example, I talk with my hands a lot. I didn't read *"Talking with your Hands 101"* to be able to learn how to talk with my hands.

When you reflect on this, you realize that the way people with Asperger's learn social skills that are real and genuine (and not a flow chart of "If they do this then say that"), is the same way everyone else learns social skills. Through observation and mimicry. The problem is, you need to have a certain level of awareness to do that, which means you need to be adequately out of Defense Mode, meaning you're not constantly overwhelmed by sensory input.

Finally, there's the last piece of The Sensory Funnel: the executive functioning piece. This is the last piece to "activate" because executive functioning, simply put, is the ability to "be on top of things." To organize your life, follow a plan, or a schedule, or a checklist, and get things done in a reasonable fashion. When you think about it, that takes a lot of emotional capacity, social capacity, and on top of all else, a strong need to not be internally freaking out 24/7. It's hard to maintain and follow a schedule when you are deep in Defense Mode.

So how do you use this information in your life? Where should you start?

A lack of social skills is a symptom of being too overwhelmed and in Defense Mode. And until you get somebody with Asperger's out of Defense Mode, you won't be able to teach them social skills. It's like taking somebody in Iraq that's involved in an active battle and saying, "Hey, do you want to learn how to knit?" While they may want to make sweaters, they have more important things on their mind. They're just trying to stay alive.

So until you can get them to where they are not just trying to stay alive, where they are calm and able to take in more life instead of being in Defense Mode—survival mode all the time—then they won't really

PART ONE: SELF

learn anything. You can teach them all the social and executive functioning skills you want, but they will not be receptive to them until you deal with the sensory, emotional, and awareness pieces first.

My Story

The Beginning: Getting Stuck and Not Fitting In

Let me ask you a question: Do you ever feel like you don't fit in? I felt that way when I was a kid. I was the twelve year old that was happy browsing a forum about a video game. That was my idea of a fun time. Obviously, I didn't have many friends. I didn't go out and do many things. I stayed in and was on the computer.

My world was the computer, and if you took me away from what I knew, I was really sad and really depressed.

As I said, I was diagnosed with Asperger's when I was twelve and people always ask me "What was it like being diagnosed with Asperger's?" Well, one day I was playing computer games, and then the next day my mom came in and said, "Hey, you have Asperger's."

I just thought, "Can I get back to my computer game now?" But underneath I was so confused and scared about life, my future, and my ability to "succeed." There was nobody to say, "What you're feeling is real." There was nobody to say, "It's OK to feel this." There was nobody to say, "Here, let me teach you how to do life.".All they cared about was what year Rome fell and different types of verbs. The stuff that, to be honest, I couldn't care less about.

See, when you are trying to survive and get through the day, you don't have the time or emotional capacity to care about different verb types or really anything else that is in the school system.

That was the start of the decade of my life where I was shut down. I was defensive. I was disconnected. Defense Mode robs you of your humanity, because you feel like you want to connect to people, but you're so internally scared of every single sensation that there's this gnawing emotional hole and all you can do is constantly try and compensate for it, avoid the world, and defend against anything that comes near . . . even things that you wouldn't normally need to defend against, such as a pen. If it makes you uncomfortable at all, if there's any uncomfortable sensation, you want nothing to do with it.

So this is what I was like for a decade of my life. I was in this defensive state. I was in this stuck state, and I was scared.

Defense Mode affected me on more than just a fear level. It affected me biologically, psychologically, emotionally, and prevented me from having a full life. As someone with Asperger's, you can try to do life all you want, but you're never going to flourish and thrive until you are out of Defense Mode.

The answer to getting out of Defense Mode isn't complicated. Defense Mode is a state where you are extremely stressed out. The way to get out is to reduce that stress. The concept is simple. The implementation requires consistency, similar to working out. The concept of a push-up is easy. The magic lies in the consistent implementation.

By the way, there is no permanent state of "out" when it comes to Defense Mode. Sometimes you are out, sometimes you are in. The goal is to minimize the time you are in and be able to get out quickly.

As far as I'm aware, the only way to permanently avoid stress, anxiety, and emotional intensity is to be dead. That isn't our goal. Our goal

PART ONE: SELF

is to be resilient against stress so that we can deal with it effectively and efficiently when it shows up in our lives.

So, I progressed through middle school (somehow), and then I started high school.

Sometimes, my high school teachers would take me aside and say, "Danny, you really need to stop asking questions, because in the real world people won't accept that, and you aren't going to go far in life."

Once, during one of my IEP (Individualized Education Plan) meetings, the special education director sat down with us and said, point blank, "Danny's probably not going to do much in life. He's probably just going to go to City College. And he's probably just going to go work a part-time job and live at home."

So first of all, screw him.

Who is he to dictate what I will and will not do in life? It really frustrates me when someone takes away another person's hope like that. I've heard countless stories from our community like "When my kid was five, the doctors told me he would be retarded and never even learn to walk or hear us."

I've also seen a few TV specials that claim that people with Asperger's don't have empathy or emotions, and therefore, they're just an automaton.

So I checked out. I decided I was done. So done that in my senior year of high school, I actually ended up just working in a computer lab that, fun story, I didn't even get assigned to. It was there, it needed fixing, and no one else was doing it. I ended up being a self-proclaimed IT guy and setting up all the things. I was in that computer lab every single day of the week, sometimes on Saturdays, too, just fixing things, configuring things. It was this giant mess. There was a Mac OS X 10.5 server sitting in the corner that nobody was using. Students didn't have a good way to login or access their files. So some days, instead of going to English class or chemistry, I ended up working in that computer lab, and no one stopped me because at that point all of my teachers realized that soon I would be out of their hair, and it was easier to let me do my thing as long as I maintained my grades.

My Life with Video Games

Growing up, I spent the majority of my free time playing video games. It was my social life. It was how I learned about the world. It was how I explored different sides of my personality and how I satisfied my curiosity.

When I wasn't allowed to play video games, I was reading books about video games, designing video games in my head, and talking about video games. It seemed to others that I was addicted because that was all I would focus on. But, on the inside, I was learning new vocabulary. I was hanging out with friends in the online world. I was creating a safe place to explore what it means to be a human. I was processing the day's events. I was just having fun and exploring and, most importantly, I was actually having an active, engaged, thoughtful, learning experience that contributed a large part to my growth and development. It made me the person I am today. I think a lot of parents don't see the positive benefits of video gaming. All they see are the "evils" and the negative side, not how video gaming can be a viable, rewarding hobby (or an extremely lucrative career path).

I've seen videos of dads running over their kid's video games with a lawnmower "for their own good!" Great way to destroy all the trust you have with your son, Dad!

PART ONE: SELF

Look, video games have good aspects and bad aspects, just like anything in life. When most people worry about "balance" in terms of playing too many video games, they have a few very valid points, wrapped up in a lot of misunderstanding and fear.

I don't believe that there is such a thing as "too much video gaming." I do believe (and the science easily supports this) that there is such a thing as too much sitting and too much staring at a screen.

Too much sitting leads to extremely stiff muscles and a lack of physical coordination. I'm not a physical therapist here to tell you why moving is important, but if you want all the details I'd suggest asking one.

Too much staring at a screen can lead to A) trouble going to sleep because the blue light of the screen tricks your body into thinking it is still daytime, and B) nearsightedness, which can make it harder to see in general.

Beyond that, the question I ask myself every day is "Is this serving me? Am I genuinely doing this because I want to, or because I'm bored?"

I realized that after almost two decades of playing video games, killing virtual people no longer appealed to me. Building things no longer appealed to me. (Last time I played Roller Coaster Tycoon I was so focused on it I started to dream about it.) So I stopped, and filled my time with other, more enjoyable activities.

It took me many years of being an adult to come to these conclusions and make better decisions for my life, and, to be honest, I still play video games occasionally. They're a great way to connect with friends and explore my interests, but I've also realized that the real world is much more . . . real.

When I was in Defense Mode, I played video games because it

was safe. I could pause the game at any point, and if something bad happened to me, I'd just reset and try again. While the real world doesn't offer those benefits, I am much happier playing and existing in a non-video game world, assuming I have the emotional capacity to do so.

The Boat Story

I got a Boater Education Card for the state of Washington while living in Denver, Colorado, even though I'd never owned a boat, and I'd only been to the state of Washington once when I was twelve and on a vacation.. So why would I do such a thing? Why would I get a Boater Education Card for a state in which I had never lived, for a vehicle which I had never owned?

Well, it has to do with the sentence: "Do what you can with what you have." It was my goal at that time to live in Seattle and to own a boat. I got a Boater Education Card for a state in which I didn't live, for a boat I didn't have, and I had no way to get there. But I understood that the secret to life is that there is no secret. Life is just a recipe. Once you learn how to follow the recipe and have the emotional capacity to consistently implement that recipe, then it gets really easy.

The first step to any recipe is always answering the question "What do you want?" In other words, which recipe do you want to follow? I wanted the "Live in Seattle and own a boat" recipe, so I started to do what I could with what I had. Even though I didn't live in Seattle or own a boat, there were still logistics that I needed to figure out. Where would I live? Where would the boat be? What kind of boat?

So I googled where to put a boat in Seattle. I used street view to look at the location, and I went on their website. For the boat, I did hours of research on different types of boats available and picked one out.

I did all that I could with what I had because I knew that eventually I would reach my goal.

Once you know what you want, step two is to go out and get it to the best of your ability. If you really want to go after it, go after it. Get your Boater Education Card. Or if you want to learn how to cook, start cooking. Or if you want to have a girlfriend, you start talking to people. Now where a lot of people get tripped up is in the uncomfortable feelings and lack of emotional capacity. I've certainly gotten tripped up there more times than I can count, which is why I stress that it is so important to focus on getting out of Defense Mode at the same time as going after your dreams.

To give you another example: Whenever I wanted to travel somewhere, I would go on the internet and find the flight I wanted and find the hotel, and do all the work to plan the itinerary, regardless of whether I had the time and money necessary to make the trip happen, and double regardless of whether I had the emotional capacity to handle being somewhere new and eating weird food.

What that did was motivate me to do the work necessary to make the goal a reality. In today's world, the knowledge is the easy part. It's the implementation of that knowledge that gets you where you want to go.

So I got my boat, and spent many years out on the water with friends, having various boating adventures. Now I've moved on, but I always remember that boat because that was the first time I really set my mind toward something, did the work I could to achieve the goal, and eventually managed to succeed because of focus, motivation, and implementation.

Picky Eating

The Stress of Picky Eating

Growing up, I was an extremely picky eater. The list of things I ate was incredibly small: peanut butter and jelly sandwiches every single day at school, and rice, beans, grilled chicken, mac and cheese, and chicken tenders at home. That's the entire list. I didn't even eat pizza until I was twelve.

Today, I'm not a picky eater at all. I eat all sorts of foods. My friends say that I do Mexican food as a hobby, because I make my own tacos from scratch (including the tortillas). In fact, a little while ago, I made a giant feast for everybody for my birthday, which included a three-course dinner.

It is with great relief (and a ton of work) that I am now willing to try new, interesting foods and be OK with traveling and eating whatever is prepared (within reason).

How did I make the leap from A to B? It's a rather simple three-part process.

First, it involves building trust in food. Second, is learning how to cook, and third, is removing pressure. As I did all three of these parts, I became a much less picky eater and was easily, effortlessly open to trying new foods.

Building trust in food for yourself involves two specific subsets of that trust: trust that the food will not overwhelm you and trusting that it is safe. Trusting that the food wasn't going to overwhelm me was the biggest fear to overcome. Food is such a sensorily rich activity with many different smells, flavors, sights, and textures. I was afraid that if I had something complex, it would overwhelm me and stress me out. I didn't want to have too much information coming in, so I was reluctant to try new things.

And then I was also afraid that the food wasn't safe. As in, was it nonpoisonous and safe to eat? Was the milk expired? Was the chicken still good? Things like that.

In order to build trust that your food is both safe to eat and not overwhelming, you need to follow a recipe. Here it is: Trust is built through interaction, meaning you need to interact with the thing that you don't trust in order to build trust in it, and that interaction needs to have four ingredients:

The first is that your interactions with food need to be recurring. You need to interact with food more than once, ideally on an ongoing basis. That part is pretty darn easy, seeing as you have a need to eat multiple times per day!

The second is that your interactions with new foods need to be intimate, meaning that you can't have an anonymous, impersonal experience with them. There needs to be a very intimate, personable experience which, again, is really easy with food because, by its very nature, you are literally making it a part of yourself.

So the first two are very easy and happen almost automatically. The next two, however, need to be focused on.

The third is your interactions also need to be positive, meaning you come away from the experience saying, "OK, that was a positive experience!" If you struggle and push yourself, you aren't going to have

PART ONE: SELF

a positive experience and you aren't going to build trust. So throughout this process, make it easy and pleasant. If it isn't easy or pleasant, take a break.

Fourth and finally, in order to build trust your interactions need to be low-risk. Poking a piece of celery if you've never tried celery is low risk. Eating a full kale and quinoa salad if you've never had kale, quinoa, or salad isn't low risk.

Once that is done, we're onto the second phase, which is all about learning how to cook without any pressure or expectation. That means that you let your curiosity drive, and you start by cooking foods that you are interested in without the pressure to eat them or have only that food for dinner. You will make mistakes. Things will become completely inedible. It's part of the process! So have fun and make food you'd want to eat, with zero pressure to actually eat it.

When cooking food that you plan to eat for a meal, make sure you always have a backup plan. Remember: zero pressure! You don't even need to eat the food that you're cooking. All you need to do is have fun with it. Learn to cook to your comfort level, whether that's making a peanut butter and jelly sandwich or making an entire Thanksgiving dinner. Learn to cook to your comfort level without any pressure at all and no stress. So if something bad happens? Hey, whatever, you order a pizza! Or use one of the many food delivery apps out there these days.

By the way, one of my favorite ways to learn how to cook is by watching cooking shows on the Food Network. Because A) they're fun, and they're really entertaining, and B) you get to learn a lot about cooking.

One of my favorite activities was to watch *Cutthroat Kitchen* where you see four contestants do the craziest cooking things. The host, Alton Brown, will say things like "We're going to take away all the knives and utensils and pots and pans you have, and only give you aluminum foil to cook with. Good luck."

You see how these professional chefs manage to get out of these crazy situations and still make an amazing meal, and it builds trust in yourself, because if they can create a delicious meal with only aluminum foil, you can create a delicious meal with actual tools.

What Causes Picky Eating

So what causes someone to be a picky eater? Mainly, at least for me, it was a fear of overwhelm. When I was a picky eater, my number one fear was that I would be extremely overwhelmed by the sensations of the food, and I wouldn't be able to handle it.

I didn't trust in my body's ability to handle the taste, or the corresponding panic that came after that. I needed to feel in control, and I didn't get that feeling when eating new foods.

Since food is so personal to everyone, it is very easy to use it as your means for control because you can just refuse to eat certain foods. That's why you see people go on hunger strikes, and that's why people are picky eaters—because it's very easy to exert control over that area of your life. Therefore, getting out of picky eating has two guiding rules: Don't overwhelm, and be in control.

I want to note here the difference between picky eating and a food preference. Picky eating is, "Do you like fish? No? Have you tried it?" "No." And a food preference is, "Do you like fish?" "Yeah, I tried tuna once. I just didn't care for it. I didn't like the taste of it."

The distinction is that it has nothing to do with the actual food itself. Picky eating is not about a like or dislike of the food. It is about

PART ONE: SELF

being scared and emotionally overwhelmed of what will happen if you eat the food. It's just another manifestation of Defense Mode.

So if the two guiding rules of getting out of picky eating are don't overwhelm and be in control, that means that you should practice cooking often, but be in control and start small with micro- commitments. If the idea of doing Thanksgiving dinner is overwhelming, then you break it down into smaller, more manageable chunks.

If the idea of making a glorious sandwich is too much for you, make peanut butter and jelly. If the idea of even using any heat is too much, start by boiling water and making pasta because that's a very good place to start. You don't need to play with the oven and high temperatures, just start small.

There is no rush. Don't overdo it. Don't overwhelm. In time, you'll find the utter joy in food, as I have.

Hygiene

On Hygiene and Cleaning Thyself

Ok, I'm just going to come out and say it: I hate dentists. Seriously, the equipment they use feels like it comes out of a medieval torture chamber, and nothing else gets as close to "Sensory Hell" for me.

In fact, I really don't like the whole Hygiene-Industrial Complex (if that isn't a thing, it is now!). It's taken me almost thirty years to get used to and like using soap, shampoo, toothpaste, deodorant, etc.

We've all heard the lectures on why hygiene is important (and can probably recite them verbatim by now . . . thanks Mom!), but until I discovered a few things I'm about to share with you, hygiene was a constant struggle (and sometimes a source of shame) for me.

Here's what finally helped me do what I know I needed to do, without it being sensory hell:

Understand The Science: There's obviously a TON of well-documented, solid scientific evidence about hygiene and cleanliness out there. There's also a lot of hearsay and bad information that has been passed down from generation to generation. So start with a completely open mind, and ask the almighty google the questions you need to answer for yourself.

Why do we need to brush our teeth? Why is shampoo important to use every day? (Hint: Google "no poo movement" (heh). There's a large amount of science to show that, depending on the person, you don't need to shampoo every day).

A few more questions to consider: Is taking a shower every day even a good idea? Does rolling around in the dirt have benefits? What are the detriments to having a cluttered room (beyond the obvious)?

Once you start to understand the actual science vs what parents and society say, then you can begin to sort out what you actually need to do to take care of yourself.

Use The Scientific Method: First, define your objective: Is it to get your parents off your back? Smell better? Finally get a girlfriend or boyfriend? Be sick less often? Be less stressed? Pick one (or more than one). Then, break it down into its parts. For example: If I want to not smell bad anymore, I'd start to do research to break down what actually causes me to smell. Then I'd create a hypothesis about what will help reduce my smell using what's called the "minimum effective dose."

What that means is, what is the minimum amount of time and energy I need to put toward showering to achieve my goal? Then you conduct an experiment to test that hypothesis and document the results. For me, it turns out I only need to shower three times weekly when I am at home and not doing strenuous activity.

This also works to test what makes hygiene activities easier for you. For example: I use a honey mango body wash for hair and body because I like the way it feels and smells. There's a certain sunscreen I like that doesn't feel greasy at all. I use tooth powder instead of toothpaste because I prefer how it feels. So get funky! Try different things!

Maybe you need a towel warmer to make the act of bathing a pleasant experience. Maybe you need a specific kind of toothbrush. Or maybe you just need more knowledge and a bit more motivation.

PART 2:

Emotional Capacity

Defense Mode

What is Defense Mode?

I remember that when I was diagnosed with Asperger's at age twelve, I went up to a few teachers and basically told them either, "You're fat" or "You suck at teaching."

I wasn't doing this to be mean. In fact, I thought I was being helpful. I was just so deep in Defense Mode that I was unaware of the impact of my actions.

So lets talk about Defense Mode. What is it? How do you get into it and how do you know if you're in it? Simply put, Defense Mode is a state in which your fight or flight system is engaged almost 24/7. You are constantly defensive, hence the name. You're constantly looking for threats and you're constantly exhausted, because all of your energy is spent protecting yourself against these threats (whether they are real or imaginary).

Defense Mode has a large biological component, a large psychological component, and a large emotional component. In the biological sense, Defense Mode is a deep state of fight or flight. In other words, you're really, really scared. Because people with Asperger's tend to be so easily overwhelmed by the sensations of the world (internal and external), our brains start to perceive the outside world in general as a threat. If sensations as a whole are overwhelming, and the world creates sensation, then it makes sense that you'd be scared and defensive against the world.

Our defense mechanism against this world of overwhelming sensation is simply to disconnect. To create our own realities and live in there because, after all, it is much safer!

So the trick is, we still need sensation in the world, it just needs to be controlled sensation. That's why, for example, loud music can be overwhelming . . . unless you are in full control of it. Then loud music can be exhilarating (and you might listen to the same song fifteen times in a row!)

The long-term problem is that when you are in Defense Mode you can never truly feel safe, because you only authentically feel safe when you can connect with other people and they can reassure you. But if you are in a state in which your social engagement systems (your facial expressions, awareness of other's emotions, knowing what to say) aren't working properly, then it is really hard to connect to other people.

So for a lot of people with Asperger's, they crave connection more than anything on the planet, but the neurology of their body is working against them and makes it near impossible for that to happen.

Instead of being calm, receptive to new experiences, and able to process whatever the day throws at you, in Defense Mode you are always in this semi-fearful, alert, hyperactive, nervous, vigilant state.

When you are in Defense Mode, you try to control every single action in order to feel safe, because the only way you can feel safe is to know what to expect. If you don't know what to expect, then the uncomfortable feelings that you've spent your whole life trying to avoid appear again.

When I was in Defense Mode the most (during my teenage years) it was a giant struggle for my parents to get me to do anything I didn't

PART TWO: EMOTIONAL CAPACITY

want to do. Internally, I was so terrified of any sensation in my body because I was wound so tight that I shut down at anything new or different. So I spent the majority of the time just playing on the computer and waiting for something to change.

As I transitioned to young adulthood, the majority of the time I just didn't have the emotional capacity to handle everything I needed to do in a given day. So, by necessity I had to ignore certain things because I just didn't have the energy. Things like making dinner, or doing all of my schoolwork. I wanted to do them, I just didn't have the available emotional capacity to handle doing them.

Life became a depressed, anxious struggle. In my head I was thinking "I'm scared of what's going to happen because I don't trust in my own ability to handle it, and I don't feel any connection."

If you stay in Defense Mode long enough, then the comorbidities start to come up as well. Things like panic attacks, severe, crippling anxiety, or deep depression and a lack of motivation.

So that's Defense Mode in a nutshell. If you'd like to understand the science, I highly suggest you read *In An Unspoken Voice* by Dr. Peter Levine and *Reframe Your Thinking Around Autism* by Holly Bridges. Both revolutionized my understanding of myself, and I hope they do for you too.

What It Feels Like to Be in Defense Mode

When I was deep in Defense Mode, it felt like I was constantly overwhelmed. It felt like I was constantly being attacked. Every single little thing, whether or not it actually had a logical, rational basis for being threatening, changed and colored my entire perspective. So for example: A pen could be threatening in Defense Mode, not because somebody is throwing it at you, but just because it is there, and seeing it triggers you in some way.

In Defense Mode, I often felt the need to control and keep everything exactly as it was because I was so overwhelmed that anything new just added to the overwhelm and shut me down even further.

So I was in a constant state of fear and shut down, withdrawing further and further away from the world. I got depressed, I got anxious, and it made it hard to accomplish basic functions in the world. When I was deep in Defense Mode, it literally shut down the parts of me that I needed to function in everyday life. Things like focusing, executive function, digestion, social skills, etc. So I felt like I was broken. Then on top of that, I started to question what that meant for me as a person. Am I a good person? Do I have worth?

It's really hard to learn social skills, executive functioning skills, or really any other life skills until you get out of Defense Mode, and until you get out of Defense Mode, it will be almost useless to try and learn because you will not be in a receptive state. It's like throwing sand into the ocean. You're not going to build an island anytime soon from doing that.

So Defense Mode is caused by constant overwhelm from four main sources. First, we have overwhelm in terms of your feelings and your sensations. That means the five senses, but also the internal sensations that your body produces as well as your reactions and responses to those sensations. Then there's overwhelm from the environment, both the physical built space, and the expectations that the space holds. For example, you might not be overwhelmed by the physical architecture of a school building, but the expectations that building contains can be incredibly overwhelming.

PART TWO: EMOTIONAL CAPACITY

Then there's overwhelm from relationships (or lack there of), and finally, there's overwhelm from the body and mind, like lack of sleep, poor diet, etc.

So if you reduce overwhelm in those four areas, you get out of Defense Mode. This is not an additive process. It is a subtractive one. You don't learn to add new things and then, once you add enough things, you get out of Defense Mode. You subtract things. You learn to stop fighting, you learn to allow more, you learn to reduce stress, and you learn to take better care of yourself.

It's the difference between doing surface treatments and treating root causes. If you get to the actual root of an issue and resolve it, everything upstream changes. Versus, if all you deal with is surface treatments, then you may never change the root cause, and the problem will always remain there.

Another example would be painting a rusty bicycle gold and calling it beautiful. No, it's still a rusty bicycle. You just painted it gold. As opposed to working to get off all of the rust, and making it shine like new, and then painting it gold.

This does require work, but the thing is, painting the rusty bicycle gold is only fooling yourself. It doesn't actually get you the result that you want. When you do the work to scrub off all of that rust and refurbish the bike, then, and only then, does it actually start to work and shine like new with no underlying issues.

So how do you get yourself out of Defense Mode? The first thing is to set your expectations properly. This is a skill, and like any skill you are going to suck at first. The sooner you accept this and embrace the suck, the faster you can get out of Defense Mode. Just like playing the piano for the first time, where no actual music comes out, there probably won't be any getting out of Defense Mode the first time you try it.

Don't give up! This is what is supposed to happen. Remember, this is a skill. Embrace the suck. After practicing for a few weeks, you'll start to feel what is, in my opinion, the most heavenly feeling on earth: relaxation.

With that being said, here's the basic idea behind getting out of Defense Mode: You are really, really, really stressed. So we need to do things that are really, really, really relaxing AND things that remove the stress you already have. In other words, we need to do self-care (relaxation) and emotional processing (removing stress you already have). There's more on that in the "Stress and Self-Care" section.

Going Back into Defense Mode

Don't let the simpleness of this process fool you. This doesn't need to be complicated. As we say often at AE, getting out of Defense Mode is about doing one thing ten thousand times, not doing ten thousand different things. The thing is, there is no true "out" for Defense Mode. At least not permanently. THIS IS NOT A BAD THING! It just means you are alive, because the only way to experience zero stress, and thus zero Defense Mode, is to be dead. That would be bad.

All we need to do is keep in mind that in the process of getting out of Defense Mode, you're going to get out and then you're going to go back in. At first, you'll be in Defense Mode most of the time, but then you'll finally feel like you've gotten your head above water and can relax.

Then you'll start to feel Defense Mode creep back up on you. The trick is, fighting that feeling of going back into Defense Mode is just going to cause Defense Mode to happen more often. Remember:

PART TWO: EMOTIONAL CAPACITY

Defense Mode is about being stressed, so the trick to getting out is to relax and do self-care, not to go to war with yourself.

Over time, the ratio of in/out of Defense Mode changes. I'd say that I am out of Defense Mode 80 percent of the time these days. That doesn't concern me at all because I know that when I go back into Defense Mode, it's just an indicator that I am really stressed and need to take a break. When I take that break and take time to relax, calm down, and soothe myself, I get out again and can continue on with my life.

Depending on how deep you are in Defense Mode, it may take a little while to feel relaxed the first time. For me, it took awhile. So be patient, and go slow.

Think about it like this: Imagine you have no idea how the process of exercise works. The whole concept is completely unknown to you, and you are really weak. So I come along and say "Hey, I have a method to increase your strength!" So I teach you how to do push-ups, and they are really hard and painful, but you trust that somehow this is going to make things better.

The next day you wake up and are extremely sore and extremely pissed off that not only did it not work, it made things worse. Obviously, if you know the science of exercise, you know that it did work, but the way it works is completely different than you first thought.

Defense Mode works in similar ways. Getting out of Defense Mode is not linear. It's not something where you can expect to gain 5 percent capacity each week. It's an exponential experience. The more you do it, the more results you get.

There's nothing to be ashamed of here. Defense Mode is literally an injury. A nervous system that is so hypervigilant and overworked that it stops working properly. It is a perfectly normal response to an abnormal situation.

Stress and Self-Care

The Secret to Resolving Big, Overwhelming Feelings

This is the story of how I had cataclysmic level panic attacks and my realization of how to stop them.

When I say cataclysmic level, I mean I was curled up in a fetal ball on the floor screaming "I don't want to die" while meanwhile it was a bright, sunny day with zero threat.

Another time, I was on an airplane and absolutely convinced that, for whatever reason, I was going to fall through the airplane to my death. It was such an absurd notion that I could even logically see that the laws of physics would not change just for me, but my body didn't seem to get the message. So I just sat in extreme panic until the plane landed.

Every night in my apartment in Seattle, as the sun would set, a massive amount of panic would set in, and I didn't know how to handle it. Everything I did seemed to make it worse.

I remember being out on my boat with some friends, with everything seeming OK externally, but internally I was freaking out and barely holding it together. It was really bad.

A few months later a group of us went to go see *How to Train Your Dragon 2* in theaters, and about three-quarters of the way through the movie, I was wrestling with my own anxiety internally like I always did . . . and then something changed.

Before, the thoughts were always "Fight the anxiety, fight the anxiety, fight the anxiety, I should be able to do something!

I should not have anxiety. I am feeling anxious. But I shouldn't feel anxious. But I shouldn't feel that I'm feeling anxious. So now I'm just stupid, but I know that I shouldn't feel that I'm stupid, and then just more anxiety. Now, I feel guilty for feeling all of these things. And I'm just stressed out. But I shouldn't even feel stressed out."

That was my normal loop, which happened pretty much every waking hour. It got to the point where I would be grateful for the first five seconds I was awake, because that part of my brain hadn't booted up yet and I had some momentary peace.

So anyway, about three-quarters of the way through the movie I remember thinking, "I'm done. I refuse to play this game anymore. I'm not going to do the game of trying to fix and resist my anxiety anymore. I quit. If my anxiety overwhelms me and kills me, then so be it. But I am done."

And the weird thing is . . . As soon as I had that thought, the anxiety stopped pretty darn immediately.

The profound realization I had during the movie is that the thing I was calling anxiety wasn't the sensation of overwhelm and panic I felt. It was the response of me trying to suppress how I felt, and control it, and deny it, and fix it.

Once I stopped denying it, stopped resisting it, and stopped trying to fix it . . . the anxiety went away.

I was sitting there in the movie and thinking "There's the feeling, cool. It's getting bigger. It's getting bigger. It's getting bigger. It's getting bigger.". . . and then it crested, like a wave. . . . and the anxiety was gone.

PART TWO: EMOTIONAL CAPACITY

Think about this for a second. What if the most wise, loving, attuned response that you could give yourself was to do nothing? Not some old, cold, uncaring, resigned "I give up" feeling.

But instead a loving, caring, holding response.

What if the wisest thing to do is to realize that it is the abandonment of these feelings that causes the anxiety, and to invite them back in, rather than trying to suppress them? To invite them back into you, rather than trying to get rid of them, control them, change them, tweak them, suppress them, ignore them, deny them.

During that movie, I realized the answer was to stop playing the game entirely. Stop fighting the anxiety. Realize that, yes, occasionally you'll have feelings that get a little bit big, but they will never be more than big feelings until you resist them.

The dominant western cultural story isn't helpful here. It says, "You shouldn't feel that way. Feelings are bad. Feelings are evil. Don't let your emotions get the best of you. Don't feel angry. Don't be sad. Be happy. Don't feel this way. Feel that way.

Some feelings are bad. Some feelings are good. You shouldn't feel the ones that are bad. If you are feeling the ones that are bad, don't. And if you continue to, then it's a character judgment and a moral failing on your part."

But what we've taught ourselves as a society is to just disconnect, drink, take drugs. Do what you need to do, so you don't feel the pain. Look at your phone!

"Feelings are bad. If you have a headache, don't go and fix the headache. Don't figure out what's wrong. Just take Tylenol, and you don't even notice you have a headache. And then you're good," our culture says.

However, the answer to those overwhelmed feelings is to go toward them, and allow the feelings to happen, and let your body take over and do what it does best.

Our body has an inbuilt uncomfortable feeling resolution mechanism. It has a way of emotional regulation that works without you having to do anything. In other words, your nervous system already has a way to deal with and resolve those big feelings.

If you've ever watched *Scooby Doo*, you know what I'm talking about. Shaggy and Scooby are always shaking in fear. So here's my question to you:

Why shaking? Are they cold?

As it turns out, the shaking is our nervous systems way of resolving the pent-up energy that comes from overwhelm. If it is allowed to take its course, then those feelings get resolved. If you'd like to know more, I'd highly suggest reading *The Revolutionary Trauma Release Exercises* by Dr. David Bercelli and *In An Unspoken Voice* by Dr. Peter Levine.

How To Connect To Yourself

What I want you to do right now is get in a comfortable position, and just notice how you're feeling. Check in with yourself and your body. Is your stomach gurgling? Do you have a little pain in your shoulder? What's going on? For example, as I write this, my throat hurts a little bit, and my back aches slightly. So I'm just going to check in and notice those things.

And then instead of trying to fight it, instead of messing with my shoulder to try and fix it and put it in the right position, instead of trying to suppress the fact that my throat hurts a little bit, instead of trying to hold my back in a different position, I'm just going to invite those sensations in.

PART TWO: EMOTIONAL CAPACITY

I'm going to notice that I feel a little bit of anxiety. It's in the back of my neck there. I'm just going to invite that feeling in. I'm just going to allow it to happen. I'm just going to observe it, and not try and change it, not try and do anything other than just allow it and invite it in.

And as you do that, what you'll notice is that your body begins to reset itself on its own. You begin to feel a little bit better. You may feel a little bit overwhelmed at first, depending on how big the sensation is. But then things get easier, mainly because you stopped fighting it.

So whenever I feel anxious, whenever I feel disconnected, whenever I feel stressed, I take a moment. I stop. And I reset myself and allow my feelings to happen.

So here's my life now. I'm relaxed. I enjoy life. I have a thriving friend group, and life is good. Now, there's still the occasional panic attack, but the difference is that it no longer affects me at all.

About a month ago, I woke up in the middle of the night after having a dream more terrifying than any I'd had since I was thirteen. Just completely confused. I didn't know where I was and I was in a completely different mindset. I felt that same feeling I used to feel when I had daily panic attacks, like I literally could die at any moment. The floor is lava, and I just don't have any ground to stand on.

But rather than a multiple hour event, the actual panic attack took about one minute.

And then four minutes later I thought, "I'm going back to bed," and I did.

So there's the difference right there: I'll still have the panic, I'll still freak out about it, but it won't be this three-hour massive event. It will just be this small little blip and then no residual effects at all.

Advanced Allowing

I wanted to go back to the story of my terrible panic attacks I mentioned in the "How to Resolve Big, Overwhelming Feelings" section.

Remember, these panic attacks were bad. Every night as the sun would go down, I would send myself into a massive, full-blown, cataclysmic, "I could die at any moment" panic attack. And it was miserable.

I'm talking cataclysmic-level destruction at any moment. And I thought I was going to literally die. Now rationally, that's utterly absurd, but that's the level of panic attack that I was experiencing. It was clouding my vision and my judgment so much that one time when I was on a plane, I thought I was going to fall through the airplane: as if the laws of physics were going to stop applying, and I was going to fall through the seat fabric, through the underbody of the plane, and out. And that's completely not how physics work. But that's the level of panic attack and irrational fear that I had.

I would always fight with myself, too, trying to push down the anxiety, trying to manipulate the anxiety, trying to change the anxiety. Trying to say I shouldn't be this way, and trying to fix it in any and every way imaginable. It was like, I know all the personal development techniques. I should be able to get rid of my anxiety, because anxiety is the enemy, and I will crush the enemy!

And so I would push it down. I'd resist it. I'd fight it. I'd try to manipulate it and change it. And nothing worked.

And then one day, I was going to see *How to Train Your Dragon 2* with some friends in theaters . . . and everything changed.

So here's what I learned from that night. Your body has a natural, inbuilt trauma resolution mechanism. For any sort of stress, discomfort, anxiety, trauma, etc, your body has an inbuilt self-regulation mechanism to get rid of all of that stuff and bring you back to a state of homeostasis, bring you back to a state of regulation. . . . if you let it happen.

So imagine you're on the sidewalk watching cars go by and you say, "OK, there's a car. There's a car. There's another car. Oh, there's a really, really ugly car! No, I don't want to deal with that at all!"

So you get in the middle of the street and say. "Stop! I don't want to see you anymore!" But now you're staring the car down, and you are going to continue to see it until you get out of the way and let it continue on its way, so that it gets out of your field of vision.

It's the same thing that happens when you have any uncomfortable feeling. The reason why I was having so many panic attacks is because when my body would try to get rid of the panicky feeling and resolve the anxiety, I would have to feel it, and then I would go and resist that and tell my body to stop. But by saying, "Stop! I don't want feel or see these feelings!" I was preventing the feeling from actually getting out of my way and letting me move on.

To put it another way, just be. Allow. Be the lightning rod and let it go through one side and out the other. Don't resist. Just observe your feelings. Let it happen.

The more that you allow and observe, the better it gets. Because then your body knows what to do. Let your body handle it and just go along for the ride.

I got so scared with the panic attacks and anxiety because I thought if I just allowed it, it would never end. Unless I did something about it, it was going to continue forever. That's just simply not the truth. It continued for about thirty seconds, and then it stopped for good.

So for me, this has profound implications. All you need to do is be with it. All you need to do is just sit there and hold yourself. Soothe yourself. Treat yourself right.

And your body will actually resolve its own uncomfortable feelings and traumas. You don't need to control it. You don't need to fix it. You don't need to do anything, except be with the feeling.

Now, sometimes, if you have trouble being with the feeling, you may want somebody to help you go through that process, like a somatic therapist. I've had to hire many many therapists over the years, and I've found the most personal success with somatic-based therapists. If you are in the Bay Area of California, I highly recommend looking up Eva Angvert-Harren (www.evaangvert.com), whom I have used extensively and can vouch for.

So right now, let's try thirty seconds of allowing your feelings. What I want you to do is just notice whatever in your body naturally brings your attention to it. For me, right now it's my lower back. So I'm just going to notice my lower back. I can encourage you to do the same thing. Just notice what you're feeling.

And don't try and change it at all. Don't try to do anything. Don't try to manipulate it, or control it, or mess with it at all. Just simply observe it and give it space. And what you'll notice is that as you observe it and give it space, it may start to change a little bit. And just observe that and notice that, too.

So what happens for me is as I notice what I'm noticing, and simply observe and let it happen, that pain in my lower back is now mostly gone. And so things shift and change and move on their own, and you don't actually need to do much. All you need to do is stay with the feeling.

So in short, in order not to feel anxious, you need to FEEL anxious. In other words, if you are feeling anxious, you feel the anxiety,

PART TWO: EMOTIONAL CAPACITY

you observe it, you let it go through your system and you don't try and manipulate or control or force or coerce or change at all.

After you practice this new way of thinking, you slowly go back to trusting yourself. You know what to do. You know how to do it.

And if you don't, then the how isn't the hard part. In today's age of YouTube and Google the how is never the hard part. If you don't know how to do something, you go and you Google it and you find out.

The hard part is the emotional capacity to actually implement the thing. Because to do that, you need to take in the information, and then think about it, and feel it, and act from that new place with new knowledge and a new perspective. If you change your perspective, then things change.

If you're at a place where you're always so uncomfortable and trying to hold on because you don't know how to emotionally regulate, like all those anxieties that I had, then you're never really going to implement what you know. You'll just keep waiting and convincing yourself that you don't know how yet, because it's so much easier just to admit that you don't know how than to admit that you're scared.

Now, on the other hand, if you genuinely don't know how, go and learn. Go to the library. Go to Google. Type in how to do the thing, and follow the instructions. And then, go and implement.

When I first moved to Seattle I wanted friends more than anything else, and until I started to find my own internal connection to myself, friends were hard.

All the external connection stuff, connecting with friends, connecting with people, making relationships, not feeling so alone, is more about connecting with yourself first.

Because you could have a ton of people surrounding you, let's say in a room of one hundred people, and you can still feel alone because you aren't able to feel the connection to the other people, literally. If you're saying that feelings are bad, you'll reject the feeling of feeling connected to other people.

And then you'll think "I still don't feel like I have friends. I still feel alone," even though you may be in a community of thousands of people. Whereas if you're connected to yourself, it's very easy to go out and meet people and say, "Hi!"

Dealing with Stress at Home

Starting in middle school, about when I was diagnosed with Asperger's, I started to get really stressed out once I got home from school. It became a problem for my parents to get me to do homework while at the same time honoring my need to unwind and have that decompression time.

What they ended up doing (and what has worked really well ever since) was following this after-school/work schedule that we created through trial and error. Here it is:

The biggest thing that makes this schedule work is the understanding that people do the best they can with the emotional capacity they have. So if you want to do better, you need more emotional capacity. That's why this schedule starts with one hour of non-electronic decompression time. It allows you to unwind without getting subjected to the endless draw of the internet.

Many people that we talk to on a daily basis don't understand the difference between recreational time and relaxation time. Both are good. Both are necessary. Confusing one for the other leads to what I call "The Tylenol Problem."

PART TWO: EMOTIONAL CAPACITY

See, when you take Tylenol, it doesn't really make the source of your pain go away. What it mostly does is remove your ability to measure if you are in pain or not. The source of the pain is still there, but under the influence of Tylenol it is very easy to forget that you haven't resolved the issue, because it FEELS like you have.

The same thing happens when you get on YouTube or Netflix or your phone. It FEELS like your stresses are melting away, but in reality, you are just being distracted from them. Your nervous system is still working overtime due to stress, and it needs that decompression time to calm down.

Think of it like a bottle of soda. If you shake it and throw it around, a lot of bubbles are produced. Once that happens, there are two ways to "calm down" the bottle of soda. You can either let it rest for a while, or open the top and let it explode all over you.

So when you are doing this non-electronic relaxation and decompression time, the focus is on NOT giving your nervous system new things to worry about and new things to emotionally process. Give it time for your "bubbles" to calm down, lest you burst.

That could be going on a walk, reading a book (my personal favorite), doing LEGO or some other project, meditating, or staring at the sky. The trick is just to make sure that you aren't giving your nervous system more to do. You've had a hard day! Give it a break!

However, there's a big problem that a lot of people with Asperger's face: Relaxing is VERY uncomfortable to them.

If we define comfort, not as the warm, fluffy pillow, but just as what you're used to and what you know, then it makes sense that the definition of discomfort is what you don't know. If you aren't used to being relaxed, you don't know it, and therefore it is very uncomfortable. . . . which makes you stressed.

So the trick is just to start small. Do a small bit of relaxation, get used to it, and then do some more. If this becomes stressful, you're doing too much at one time. Take it slow!

So how do you actually do the relaxing? Well, we're about to discuss a few different ways to relax, recharge, and do self care, but before we do it's really important that you understand this: You don't need to do every technique mentioned here. If something isn't working out for you, don't force it! Just choose a different technique! With that being said, let's get started.

The easiest way to relax, in my opinion, is meditation. There are many forms of meditation, but my favorite is gratitude. Close your eyes and think about five things you're grateful for and why. That's it. Science has found that the more gratitude you have, the better your immune system works, the better your nervous system works, the more resilient you are.

There are many other forms of meditation, such as a traditional sitting meditation, a walking meditation, and a seemingly infinite number of guided meditations that you can find on YouTube and through various apps on your phone. Again, if you find that a certain meditation technique doesn't work for you . . . don't do it! The whole idea here is to do more of what works for you, less of what doesn't, and try new things to see if they work.

Breathing exercises can also be a great way to relax. If I am really stressed, sometimes I just stop for a few moments and focus on a slow, steady exhale (like I am blowing out of a straw). I've found that to be incredibly relaxing, and it only takes about thirty seconds to a minute for me to achieve the effect.

Once you've done the non-electronic relaxation and decompression time, THEN it is time to go be productive. Do your homework

PART TWO: EMOTIONAL CAPACITY

(if you are still in an educational institution), catch up on chores, or be productive in some other way. You'll find that, oddly enough, being productive in this way is almost effortless. Why? Because you've given yourself a chance to recharge and now your body and mind are ready to participate in the world again.

Now what happens if there is no "after school" or "after work" for you? If you are between jobs, or just wondering what to do in life, and sitting on your computer a bit too much, waiting for the stress to go down or something to change so that you can finally interact with the world?

If that is the case, I'd start by doing the non-electronic decompression time right when you wake up. Be serious about it. I've found that on the days where I take care of myself as soon as I wake up, I get more done before 11am than the days where I wake up and immediately check my phone.

The ultimate source of truth on this, however, is your own experiences and experiments. So try this out for three days. See how it works for you. Take note of how you feel before and after. Try some of the exercises that come later in this book, and follow this golden rule: Do more of what works, less of what doesn't, and try new things to see if they work.

When my parents and I were first implementing this schedule, a typical day for me would be getting home and having that one hour of non-electronic decompression time where I'd literally just read a book, sometimes in the bathroom (OK, most of the time I hid in the bathroom and read). Then I would go and do my homework, and once my homework was done, THEN I would go have fun.

Now, a key tip here is to get your homework (or whatever chore you have to do) done BEFORE fun, because it's really, really hard to transition the other way. In today's world, video games and the internet are optimized to take as much attention of yours as possible and keep you doing that activity for as long as possible. Which means, while they are fun, it is also measurably harder to switch gears and tear your attention away from video games than it is from, say, raking leaves.

PART 3:

The Outside World

Stories, Perspectives and Getting Help

Is Your Definition the Same as Mine?

My parents used to come up to me and say, "Clean your room!" so I did, and then when I told my parents I had cleaned my room, they would go in and check and get mad because I hadn't cleaned my room when I said I had. Obviously, this led to immense frustration because I HAD cleaned my room and they were telling me I hadn't.

Breakdowns in communication like this inevitably lead to frustration because everybody feels like they aren't being heard and understood. This makes it even harder to communicate because you get into this self-perpetuating cycle of not feeling heard, and therefore feeling like you need to really make yourself heard, and then, you blow off everyone else, which makes them listen less, which makes it even harder to communicate.

So you'd think the answer would be, learn how to communicate, right? Yes, but it depends on what you mean by communicate. Just like when my parents told me to clean my room, I learned that people can have wildly different definitions of the same word.

Before you can effectively communicate and have conversations, there needs to be a shared understanding. When you look at the word communication and its Latin root, *communis*, it means to make common.

So if you are speaking Italian and somebody else is speaking French, the first thing that you would do, if you need to work together, is create a common language. That seems obvious, right? Yet when people are speaking the same language, let's say, English, a lot of times, they still don't have a shared language. Because your version of "clean room" is entirely different from their version of "clean room."

The first thing to do, in this case, is to make sure that your version of clean and their version of clean are the same and everybody knows what "clean" means. I've heard some people actually take pictures of a clean room, mount those pictures on a poster board, and say, "This is what I mean by clean."

Obviously, this applies to more than just clean rooms. Whenever you are in a relationship with someone, whether that be a friend, family member, significant other, or Bob the deli guy, having a shared language is how we are able to communicate with one another. Obviously, English does some of this for us, but if you find yourself getting into constant arguments and never feeling heard, it might be time to back up and check that you have a shared understanding around the words, phrases, and expectations that constantly lead to those arguments.

The Stories I Told Myself

When I was twelve, I started playing a video game called *Neverwinter Nights*, which rapidly became one of my favorite games of all time. It's essentially an online *Dungeons and Dragons* role-playing game. One day

PART THREE: THE OUTSIDE WORLD

in-game I was in a tavern in the seedy little part of town and somebody beat me up in-game. When that happens, there's a sound effect when somebody clicks on your little bag to look into it. I heard that sound effect and got really pissed off that somebody had taken all of my stuff.

So once I got up, I ran over to the city guard, played by another player, and told them that somebody stole my stuff. When we went to go check, all my stuff was still there. I assumed that the player that beat me up had taken all my stuff and not just looked into it and thus, I got really frustrated and angry.

I came from one perspective and then acted according to the story I had told myself. Note the use of the word "story" here, because my assumptions were just that. Things I assumed, not based in any fact. The reality of the matter is I heard a sound effect, but I assumed someone stole all my in-game items I spent hundreds of hours collecting, and so I proceeded to get very angry.

Once I realized that I was incorrect, it hit me like a ton of bricks. I was SO SURE that the other player stole my belongings. Instead, he had just looked inside to see what I had, and ended up taking nothing.

Here's another example of the type of story I'm talking about. Imagine it's 8 pm and you've just run out of milk, and you don't have time to go to the store in the morning. So you send someone from your household to go get the milk at the grocery store and they say, "Ok, I'll be back at 9 pm. It's just going to take me a while to get the milk, but I'll be back soon."

Now it's 9:30, and they still aren't back, so you try calling them, and you try texting them. No answer. So you start to panic.

Now it's 10 pm and they still aren't back, and your mind is racing, asking "What happened? What does this mean?" Since you have no data, you start making up stories and guessing.

Maybe they got in a car accident. Maybe they were kidnapped. Maybe they have a flat tire. Or maybe they won the lottery.

You have literally no idea.

These are examples of assigning meanings and stories, and these are an essential part of everyday life. Can you imagine how it would be if when you had a problem or a lack of information, you couldn't just make up stories and have a best guess? We wouldn't be able to function. Stories are essential to our lives and they drive our everyday functions, everything from the alarm beeping indicating it's time to get up, to the green light signaling it's time to go, to my stomach gurgling that it's time to be hungry.

The problem is we often don't have enough data to really derive a true meaning or story, so we need to make a guess. Sometimes, those guesses can end up generating more problems.

Let's say you take a math test, and get a C on it. You could say "I suck at math," but here's the thing. You don't know that you suck at math. The only true thing you do know is that you got a C on a math test.

Obviously, you did not answer all of the questions correctly on the math test. That's the "fact." All other stories and meanings that stem from that fact could swing either way. You could say "I suck at math, therefore it is worthless to try to study," or you could equally say "I just didn't study hard enough, therefore I need to study harder next time." Both are valid, but the story that you choose greatly affects your life going forward.

The story that you choose will create a positive or negative, self-reinforcing feedback loop that can color your identity (your story of yourself) for years to come. If you tell yourself the story that you are bad at math, you won't study, and when the next math test comes around, you will get a bad grade, thus proving that you suck at math (because you didn't even try to study because it was pointless).

Now, on the other hand, if you tell yourself the story that you are good at math and just didn't study hard enough, you'll take the actions necessary to figure out where you went wrong, improve, and do better next time.

So how do you choose a story that serves you best? It starts by separating out the fact from the story about that fact. In our math test example, the fact is that you didn't get all the questions right. The story is WHY that occurred.

Once you start to practice separating out the fact from the story, you can challenge that story. What other stories could be true? Is it possible that you don't suck at math and were just having a bad day? Is it possible that other stories about yourself could be told differently?

The better you get at telling yourself stories that serve you instead of steal your power, the better off you'll be in life.

You Mean I Don't Need to Figure Everything Out from Scratch?

I remember when I found out that personal development was a thing. The phrase "personal development" has a LOT of different meanings, so what I am referring to in this context is that people have figured out how to actually be competent in all areas of life, including marriage, dating, food, finances, education, psychology, health, etc. They've figured out how to be successful in life, and they have documented each and every step of how to do it.

You want to learn how to set goals and achieve things? Cool. There are tons of books on the subject that are six hundred pages long. Go read *The Law of Success* by Napoleon Hill. You want to learn how to make money? Go read one of the ten thousand books on investing.

You know you want to have a better relationship with your friend, sister, brother, aunt, uncle, niece, wife, or husband. There are lots of books on that subject too. Beyond books, there are people whose whole career focuses on teaching this information. People like Tony Robbins, John Gray, Suze Orman, and many others who are experts in their field.

They're literally documenting each step and saying, "Here's how I got from being a homeless person to living in a mansion, and here is exactly what I did at each step, and here's how I went from being an anxiety-driven wreck to being calm, cool, and collected, and I've documented each step."

The trick, though, is believing that. I reiterate: The trick is believing in that. I didn't believe that it could work for me. I believed that, sure, the concept worked, but it didn't apply to me. But I wanted to believe them. I wanted to believe that it was possible for me to achieve my dreams. I wanted to believe that it was possible for me to do what I wanted to do.

So here's what I did: I had a seven-foot-long poster printed out and I stuck it on the wall opposite my bed so it was the first thing I saw when I woke up and the last thing I saw when I went to bed.

It says "Impossible is just a big word thrown around by small men who find it easier to live in the world they've been given than explore the power they have to change it. Impossible is not a fact. It's an opinion. Impossible is not a declaration. It's a dare. Impossible is potential. Impossible is temporary. Impossible is nothing." —Muhammad Ali

I looked at that poster every day for over two years with the belief

PART THREE: THE OUTSIDE WORLD

that if I put a different message in front of me every single day, it would begin to shape my focus.

What I found is that as I began to think about this more and more, my thoughts begin to slowly shift, but the shift wasn't big enough. I was still in college flailing, and not really knowing what I wanted to do in life, and failing a few classes. Things weren't working out too well

Eventually, though, a breakthrough happened.

I had this realization—there are people that will actually help you, and if you follow their advice it will work. That's the part I was missing. I had thought "Oh, this will work for everybody but me."

Next time you have a sticking point in life, you don't need to suffer and figure it out on your own! There are people out there in the world that would be THRILLED to help you and show you exactly what they did. They've written books, done TED talks, produced YouTube videos and more. The collective knowledge of humanity is waiting for you. The door is unlocked. All you need to do is open it.

Moving Your Life Forward

Loops of Competence

Experiential competence is one of the most valuable things you can participate in. I say experiential because, for a lot of people, the act of increasing their skill and competence level with something involves study and knowledge gathering, rather than the practical application and real world participation.

This is the concept we call "loops of competence."

What are loops of competence? Let's say, for example, that you want to run a marathon. But you've never done any exercise in your life. Studying about how to run a marathon is only going to get you so far. At a certain point, you need to go out running. However, if you just try to run a marathon on day one, that probably is going to end badly for you. It's far more useful to start with a smaller chunk (what we call a "loop"). Say, running one hundred feet.

After you master that, you can move onto a bigger loop, such as running one mile every day. Then, you continually increase the size of your loop, making sure to "complete the loop" by being successful at your assigned goal. Setting yourself a goal of running one mile and succeeding is a completed loop. If your loop isn't complete, make a smaller loop.

In other words, don't bite off more than you can chew. I see a lot of people with Asperger's declare that they want to become independent, and then try to do everything at all once immediately and crash and burn.

I fell victim to this. I declared that I wanted to make a million dollars in one month and have everything good happen in my life immediately.... when I should have started with "get a job."

I've seen so many young adults on the spectrum create a big loop and a big goal, fail, say "I can't do it!" and then internalize the failure and have low self-esteem. If that's you, that's not your fault. You just need to make your loops the right size. Start with something that you know you can't fail at.

If you want to be good at cooking, but you're afraid to cook and you don't think you can cook, toast a piece of bread. Something that is laughably easy to the point where you have no question that you can do it.

Then, try to slightly exceed that. Maybe it's time to try toasting some bread and then putting some meat and veggies on it. Boom! You just cooked and made a sandwich.

Obviously, there is more you can do with loops of competence than just make a nice sandwich. You can use this concept to get better at anything, whether it be a job or a skill or something that you feel unsure of. The point is, start small, go slow, and be consistent. Consistency wins over scale every day.

I'd recommend starting by picking one area of your life you'd like to improve, and then identify what the smallest "loop" you can do is. For example, if I wanted to focus on making friends, my smallest loop would be saying "Hi" to one new person every day. Eventually that will become easy, and you'll be on your way.

PART THREE: THE OUTSIDE WORLD

Troubleshooting When Things Go Wrong

Troubleshooting is half art and half strategy: It requires figuring out what is wrong in a system and resolving it.

In a mechanical system, that means isolating the problem part, taking it out, and replacing it. In an organic system (something that is grown, not built), that means examining the environment of the system to figure out where the issue is. For example, if you have an issue with a tree, you can't necessarily just cut that part out and replace it.

You need to look at the environment of the tree to see what's wrong. Do you need to give it more soil? Give it more nutrients? Give it more sunlight?

Obviously, this applies to more than just trees, so let's take a real life example: applying for a job. If I'm applying to a lot of jobs and getting no callbacks or interviews, then I have two choices. I can either assume that I am unemployable and no one likes me, or I can begin the troubleshooting process to figure out what is going wrong and how to fix it.

First, we need to identify the steps that happen once I apply for a job. The first step is the actual act of applying for the job and filling out the application. Then, I have to get invited to an interview. Then, depending on the company, I may have to go through a second or third round of interviews, and then I have to get offers. Once I accept one of those offers, I have a job.

Now that we've defined the steps, we need to ask, "Where do I get stuck and what feedback am I getting? Are people just not replying to me at all? Have I started to follow-up with them?"

As you start to take a look at the entire process, you can identify where the sticking point is and then begin to focus more on that area.

So let's say that I'm not getting many calls back once I fill out applications. It might turn out that the PDF I've been sending of my resume is corrupted and unreadable. Or it might be that I have several typos in my resume that I didn't catch. Or it might be that I've only applied to two jobs, which simply isn't enough.

To give you another example of how this process works, let's take a look at food. There's a process called the elimination diet, where the idea is to eliminate the foods that are known to cause issues in some people (like wheat) for a month, see how you feel, and then introduce the food back into your diet.

The thinking goes, that after a month without the food, it will be a lot easier to tell how you feel when you eat that food. So in essence, we're just doing the troubleshooting process with food. We identify the problem, remove it, gather feedback, introduce it, gather feedback and then make a conclusion from there.

Next time you get stuck and can't figure out how to proceed in life, try this process. It's simple, effective, and an extremely valuable part of how I live my life every day.

Conclusion

AS I SAID AT THE BEGINNING OF THIS BOOK, Asperger's can suck sometimes, but it doesn't need to suck forever. There are tools, strategies, and methods that you can implement to drastically improve your life, and there are people who have implemented these tools that have gotten results and drastically changed their lives. It is possible.

My hope is that the stories and tools in this book provide you a starting place on the path to change. A space where you can step back, relax, gain perspective, and move forward with the hope and motivation that it is possible to have a fulfilling life with Asperger's.

Remember: If you are stressed, focus on relaxing. If you are stuck, take a step back and change your perspective by asking questions and testing your assumptions. If you are overwhelmed, sink into the feelings instead of fighting them.

Those of us on the spectrum are blessed with unique skills, abilities, and talents, and it's time that we share them with the world. Thank you so much for reading this labor of love and putting your trust and faith in me and all of us here at Asperger Experts, and remember: People do the best they can with what they have.

If you'd like more, I encourage you to visit our website at www.AspergerExperts.com.

I hope to see you there,

Danny Raede
Asperger Experts